Leif Eriksson and the Vikings

Betty Lou Kratoville

High Noon Books
Novato, California

Cover Photo: North Wind Picture Archives
Interior Illustrations: North Wind Picture Archives
Pictorial History Research

International Standard Book Number: 1-57128-166-5

9 8 7 6
0 9 8 7 6 5 4 3

Contents

1 Erik the Red 1

2 The Teller of Tales 9

3 Leif Finds Vinland 15

4 The Brothers 22

5 The Merchant.....................................29

6 The Sister...38

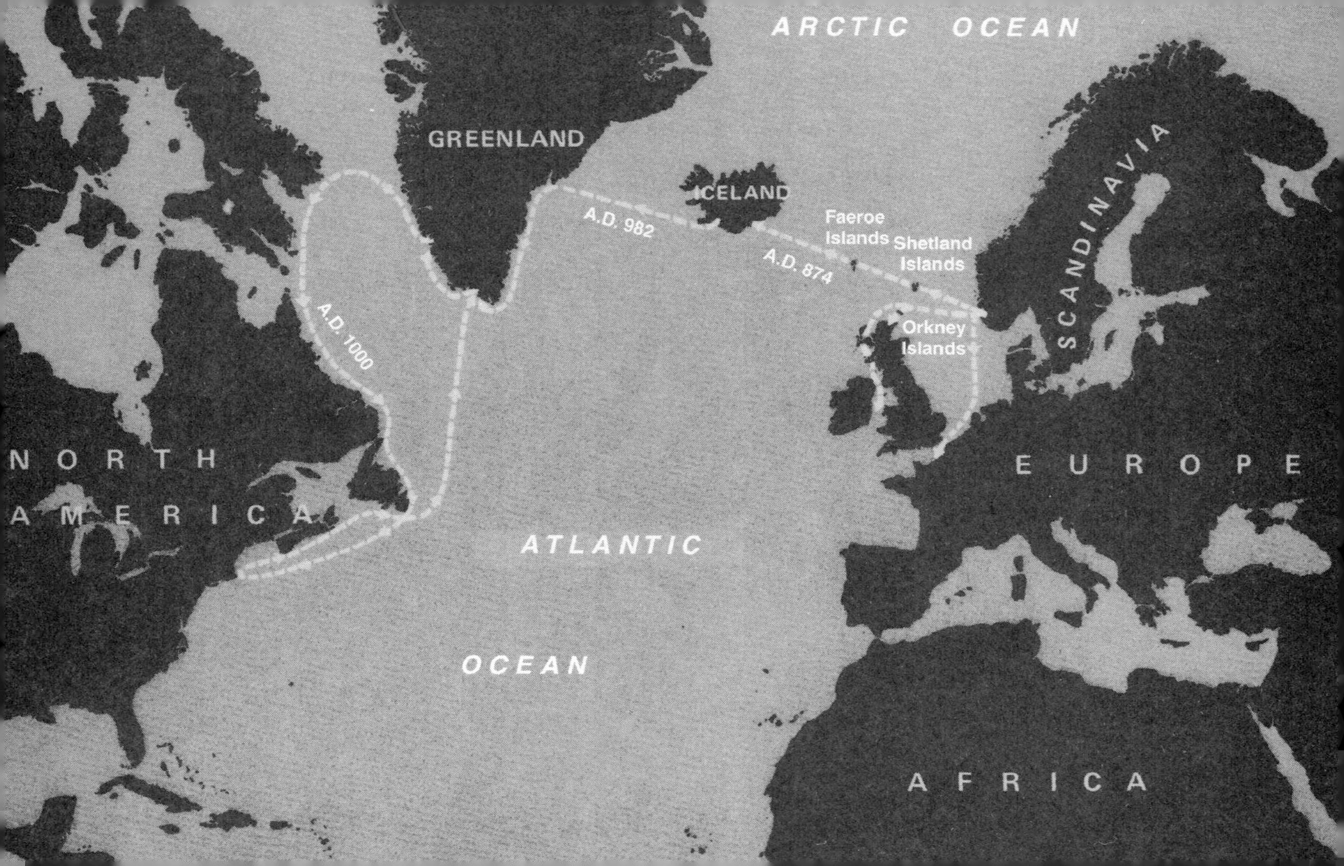

ARCTIC OCEAN
GREENLAND
ICELAND
Faeroe Islands
Shetland Islands
Orkney Islands
SCANDINAVIA
A.D. 982
A.D. 874
A.D. 1000
NORTH AMERICA
EUROPE
ATLANTIC OCEAN
AFRICA

CHAPTER 1

Erik the Red

What you are reading today comes from a *saga*. Saga means something that is *said*. It means a true story that is told over and over again. This is how people like the Vikings kept track of their deeds. Why didn't they just write about them? There was a good reason. The Vikings had a strange language called *rune*. It was very hard to write in rune. Many years later people began to use the Latin alphabet. It was then that the saga of Leif Eriksson was at last written down.

Leif's father is almost as well known as Leif. His flaming beard and hair caused people to call him Erik the Red. Erik had a hot temper. It was well known that he had killed more than one man. One day a violent act caused him to be driven from his home in Norway. He went to Iceland. A number of people he knew had already settled in this cold, wet country.

Erik soon found a wife in Iceland. It was there that his children were born. Leif was the eldest of these. As a boy, his life was spent mostly out-of-doors. He helped tend cattle and sheep. He hunted and fished and walked through the hills. The family had *thralls* (slaves) to do the rough work.

Iceland was a peaceful place. It had laws and courts. The courts were called *Things*. There were no judges. It was the Icelanders who settled scraps. There were no police. Icelandic families had to enforce their own laws. All in all, Leif thought it was a fine place to call home.

Then suddenly one day the peace was shattered. Erik was in trouble again. In a fight over some household goods, he killed two young men. He had to be punished. He was forced to leave Iceland. The court said he could not return for three years. Where to go?

Erik could have returned to Norway. He could have set out to raid the British Isles. But he was a man who craved adventure. He had heard

3

about some islands to the west. Why not go there?

Friends helped him outfit a ship. And what a ship it was! A large Viking ship was called a *knorr*. The Vikings used them for deep-sea sailing. A knorr was about 60 feet long. It was wide enough to carry cattle and horses and even an extra small boat. Its sails were square. It had only a few oar-holes for rowing.

Erik took about 30 men with him. The saga does not tell if Leif went, too. But it is likely that he did. It would have been a fine way for Erik to teach his boy about the sea.

After four days out of Iceland, Erik spotted a huge glacier. He did not know it then but his ship was on the east coast of Greenland. The Vikings could not land. There were too many high cliffs of ice and rock.

Erik turned his ship southwest. They sailed around the southern tip of this new land. What a rich and beautiful place! Plenty of safe harbors and bright green pastures. The Vikings' hearts soared at the sight of trees. Iceland was almost treeless. The thick clumps of willow and birch meant snug houses and barns as well as strong ships and plenty of fuel.

Erik named this lush country Greenland. He spent three years exploring its west coast. It became clear that the southwest tip was the best place to settle. Here he found food - fish, birds, berries, and game. He saw plenty to trade – ivory from walrus tusks, fur from seals. It was time to go back to Iceland and spread the word.

Spread the word he did. The Icelanders were eager to hear what Erik had to say. Things were not so good in Iceland at that time. There had been a famine. Many people had died. Pastures were no longer rich and fertile. Almost all the trees had been cut down. It was time to move on.

The next summer 25 ships left Iceland headed for Greenland. It was a grim trip. A great storm struck the small fleet. Eleven ships sank to the bottom of the sea. Only 400 people were left to settle in Greenland. Among these were Erik and his family.

He chose land about 60 miles from the sea

on a small inlet. He built a long narrow house with a stream running through it. The walls were six feet thick. One by one other rooms were added. Soon there was a fireplace, then a well. Barns and pastures were made ready for cattle, horses, sheep, goats, and pigs. Erik called his new home Brattahlid.

Trade with Norway began almost at once. The Greenlanders needed iron for tools. They needed grains for bread and beer. Norway traders sought strong rope made from walrus hide, rare hunting falcons, furs, and woolens.

The Vikings lived well and peacefully for about 13 years. Then Leif took a trip to Norway. While there he heard about a merchant ship that had been blown off course west of Greenland. The ship had sailed along the coast of a land never before seen or explored.

This was all Leif needed to hear. For years he and others had wondered about birds that flew in from the west. Where did they come from? It was time to find out.

CHAPTER 2

The Teller of Tales

The merchant whose saga had begun Leif's dreams about a new land to the west was Bjorni Herjolfsson. His ship traded between Norway and Iceland. It sailed on seas that were rough and dangerous during the winter. Bjorni did most of his trading in the summer months. He liked to spend the bitter winters at his home in Norway or or at his father's house in Iceland. He and his father were good friends. Bjorni feared that the old man didn't have many years left to live. So he made sure that he saw his father at least once a year.

At the end of one trading season, Bjorni set sail for Iceland. It was an easy trip. But when he got there, he found an empty house. His father was nowhere to be seen.

"Where is he?" Bjorni asked a neighbor.

"He moved to Greenland," came the answer.

Bjorni was stunned. Greenland! That was a long trip! – and a risky one. He had never made it before. It would be wise to turn around and go back to Norway. But Bjorni wanted to see his father. He made up his mind to talk to his crew.

"I am going to Greenland," he told them, "I would like you to go with me. But I will understand if you don't want to go. It will be a long hard trip."

Bjorni's crew were Vikings. They were used to long, hard trips. They all said they would go with him. In only a few days they all wished they could change their minds. Almost at once they were lost in a thick fog. A strong north wind blew them this way and that. They were hopelessly lost. In those days they had no maps or compasses to tell them where they were.

At last the sun came out. One of the crew spotted land in the distance. Bjorni sailed his ship as close to it as he could. Was this Greenland? This hilly country didn't match what he had heard about Greenland. Back to sea they went. They headed north.

Two days later the ship drew near another shoreline. "This doesn't look right to me," Bjorni said. "I heard Greenland had a big glacier. I don't see any glaciers here."

This time his crew did not agree with him. They had all been at sea a long time. They were bored.

"Let's go ashore for fresh water and wood," said their leader.

"No," said Bjorni. "We have plenty of wood and water. I want to get to Greenland as soon as we can."

He was the captain. His word was law. So the crew turned back to its duties. In a few days they passed an island. It had high mountains and glaciers.

"This land looks good for nothing," roared Bjorni. "We go on." His crew said not a word.

Sometime later they again saw land. Bjorni smiled. "This looks like what I was told about Greenland. We will drop anchor here." What luck! Bjorni's father lived nearby.

Bjorni spent the rest of that winter with the old man. In the spring he took up trading again. He worked hard for many years. At last it was time to retire. He went to live with his father in Greenland. On the long winter evenings the two men and their friends sat by the fire. It was then that Bjorni told his tales of the land in the west. It was the beginning of a new saga. A saga that passed from mouth to mouth. In time, Leif Eriksson heard it.

How was it possible, he wondered, to go so near land and not explore it? Well, he, Leif, would find that land. He would explore it. Then he, too, would have tales to tell. Tales that would be more exciting than anyone had ever told before!

CHAPTER 3

Leif Finds Vinland

Leif found a well-built ship that was for sale. He bought it. Then he went to see his father. Would Erik lead a search for a new land? Erik shook his head. He felt he was too old. But Leif would not take no for an answer. At last his father gave in. On the way to the ship, Erik's horse stumbled. As he fell to the ground, Erik sprained his ankle. In Viking lore this was a bad omen. So Erik went home to Brattahlid. Leif and his 35 men sailed out of the Brattahlid *fjord* and turned north.

After an easy voyage of 600 miles, they reached the land they were seeking. It was just as they had heard. It was covered with snow and ice, rock, steep cliffs. Leif and some crew members went ashore in a small boat. The land was flat and barren. Leif was not impressed and left quickly to set sail south and west.

The next stop was not much better. It did have one feature of great value. Thick woods! Leif called it Markland – Wood Land. Then back to sea.

At last they found a channel that led to a river. The river led to a lake. It looked like a good place to settle for awhile. Supplies were brought from the ship. Huts were built. They had chosen well. The river and lake were full of plump salmon. Wood for building and burning was nearby. They were so pleased with their site, they built one large house. It would give better shelter for the cold weather that lay ahead.

As the winter wore on, they found they really didn't need better shelter. The weather was milder than that of Greenland. There was little or no frost. Daylight lasted longer than at home. All in all, it was a very fine place to spend the winter. They had no idea where they were. It is now thought that they most likely were on the west coast of the land that today we call Newfoundland.

The men were eager to explore. Leif set some rules. Half the men would stay at camp each day. Half would go out into the countryside. No one was to go so far, he could not get back before darkness fell.

Sagas about Leif's stay in North America do not all agree. Best known is the one about a crew member named Tyrkir. This fellow was late getting back to camp one night. Leif was worried. Tyrkir was a good friend. Leif sent out a search party. They met Tyrkir coming back to camp. He was excited.

"Guess what I have found," he shouted. "Vines and grapes!" This was welcome news.

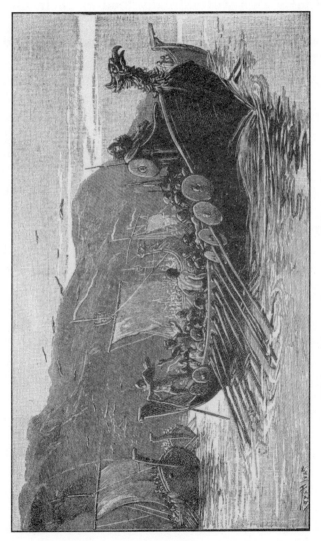

Viking ship on the coast of Vinland.

Leif's men were already loading their ship with stacks of wood. Now they could add grapes to their cargo. And the vines could be twisted into strong ropes.

Another saga tells that Tyrkir did not find grapes. He found peas or beans. Because of the odd rune language, no one can be sure which saga is correct. Leif called the place Vinland. Another puzzle! The word "vin" had two meanings. One was "wine." The other was "pasture" or "meadow." Both seem to make sense.

When winter ended, Leif pointed his ship homeward. Calm seas and sunny skies followed them all the way. One morning they sailed near a reef. Leif could see people clinging to it. They had been shipwrecked and were close to death. Leif plucked 15 men and women from that reef. Because he had found Vinland and because he had stumbled on the doomed group, Leif was called "Leif the Lucky" for the rest of his life.

Not long after he returned to Greenland, Erik the Red died. Now Leif became the leader of the people who had settled in Greenland. That meant his exploring days were over. Someone else would have to look for new lands. It was no surprise when one of his brothers volunteered to do just that!

CHAPTER 4

The Brothers

Leif had a younger brother named Thorvald. Thorvald had heard all of Leif's stories about Vinland. He wanted to try his luck there. Since Leif was now Greenland's law leader, Thorvald had to get his consent.

Leif thought this such a good idea, he let his brother use his ship. He helped outfit it with men and supplies. When all was ready, Thorvald set out with 30 men.

They reached Vinland with little hardship.

Leif's camp was still in good shape. It seemed wise to spend the winter there. It gave them time to make any repairs their ship might need.

In the spring the crew explored some of Vinland's west coast. It was lovely country with thick forests and white beaches. They did not see any sign of human life.

They returned to Vinland for another winter. The next spring they sailed their ship north and east. This land was new to them. Most likely it was Leif's Markland or what today is known as Labrador.

The first hint of trouble came when they ran into a big storm. The ship's keel broke. They had to land and spend many months fixing the keel. Back at sea, they came to a wooded land between two inlets. Thorvald and some of the crew left the ship to explore.

"This is a beautiful place," said Thorvald. "This is where I would like to make my home."

They started back to the ship. On the sandy beach they spotted three shapes. What was this? They walked closer. The three shapes turned out to be canoes. Under each canoe three Indians were sleeping. The Greenlanders did what they had always been taught to do. They pulled out their swords and spears and attacked. They killed eight Indians. The ninth got his canoe into the water. He kneeled in it and paddled with great speed. Soon he was out of range.

More was to come. That night Thorvald and his men fell asleep. The idea that they had something to fear never entered their heads. They were wrong! In the middle of the night a band of Indians attacked. This time there were more Indians than Greenlanders. Even so, no one was hurt — except Thorvald. He had been struck by an arrow under his arm. It did not look like a fatal wound. But it was. Perhaps the arrow had struck an artery. Perhaps the tip was poisoned.

The crew gathered round. Thorvald lifted his head. "Do this," he said. "Get out of here and go home as quickly as you can. But I would like to be buried on the spot I had hoped to make my home. Put a cross at my head and call it Cape Cross."

Then he died. The men sadly buried their leader. It was decided to wait until the next spring to follow his orders. The way the saga tells it, the ship sailed home loaded with grapes and vines. But with sad news for Leif about his brother.

There was yet another brother. Thorstein was even younger than Thorvald. And, like the other sons of Erik the Red, he was brave and bold. Thorstein made a vow. He would go to the place where Thorvald was buried. He

Thorvald is wounded by Indians.

would bring his brother's body home.

Thorstein was given the same ship Leif and Thorvald had sailed. But almost at once he ran into bad weather. Heavy storms tossed the ship this way and that. The crew had no idea of where they were. Just plain luck blew them into a settlement on Greenland's west coast.

They were too tired to go on. While they rested there, a plague struck the west coast of Greenland. Thorstein grew sick and died. Later his body was taken to Brattahlid. He was laid to rest near the family church.

CHAPTER 5

The Merchant

Thorfinn Karlsefni was a man of good family and very rich. He was a merchant who went from country to country. One trading voyage took him to Greenland. He spent a winter at Brattahlid with Leif Eriksson. While there he heard many tales about Vinland. This, he thought, would be a good place for people to stay and make homes.

He asked Leif if he might buy the long house and the huts at Vinland. Leif said no. He might want to use them again himself one day. No matter! Karlsefni would build his own houses.

Money was not a problem. Karlsefni had enough to outfit three ships. At least 160 men and women agreed to go with him. Karlsefni took the shortest possible route to get to the new land. His ships were loaded with people and livestock. He didn't want to risk them on the open seas any longer than need be.

They arrived safely and sailed down the west coast past Leif's Markland. Like Leif they saw great forests and many wild animals. They got their first glimpse of an Arctic fox. "What beautiful fur," said Karlsefni. "It will make a fine coat." He was, after all, a trader.

The small fleet made two or three stops along the coast of the new land. They did not find Vinland. They finally chose a spot for a settlement before winter came. The land was green and beautiful. They could see rolling hills and vast mountains.

Karlsefni unloaded his ships and put his livestock out to graze. The settlement seemed to get off to a good start. But for some reason Karlsefni had not planned well for winter. It was a hard one. Snows were heavy. Winds were biting and harsh. Hunting and fishing failed. Somehow the settlers managed to hold on until spring. Then life began to look brighter. The fish started biting. Wild game appeared. All of their livestock had made it through the winter.

Once spring came, Karlsefni wanted to try to find Vinland. He broke his crew into two groups. One group would go with him. They would head south and east. Another group would go north. Its leader would be Thorhall the Hunter. What a strange fellow! He did not speak often. When he did, he was gruff and grouchy. But he was a good hunter, and he was fearless.

Thorhall the Hunter was not happy to be looking for Vinland. Why bother? He may have made up his mind to give up the search

The merchant Karlsefni at Vinland.

and go back to Greenland. The saga about him is not quite clear. It is thought that his ship was blown off course by a sudden storm. Thorhall and his crew were shipwrecked off the coast of Ireland. They were caught, beaten, and made slaves. He was never heard from again.

Karlsefni's group sailed south for a long time. They came to a land of good pastures, forests full of game, rivers full of halibut. This rich land was almost too good to be true. Then one day nine canoes full of Indians paddled up. The two groups stared at one another. Then, without a word or sign, the Indians turned around and left. They returned to Karlsefni's camp in the spring. This time they were ready and eager to trade.

The Indians loved red cloth – big pieces, small pieces. It didn't matter. In return they swapped thick beautiful furs. All went well until one day Karlsefni's huge black bull stomped into sight. The Indians fled in a panic. When they came back, it was to fight, not to trade.

It is hard to say which side won the pitched battle that followed. But one important fact came of it. Karlsefni changed his mind. The land might be beautiful but it was too unfriendly a place to settle. He began to make plans to return to Greenland. Before leaving, he made a last try at finding Thorhall and his crew. No luck. This took so long, it was too late in the season to sail home. They had to wait until the next spring.

During that long, cold winter Karlsefni and his wife took pleasure in watching their small son grow. As far as we know, this was the first child born in North America who was not native to this land.

At last it was spring and time for the trip home. Karlsefni's ship made it safely. The other ships sank in an Atlantic storm.

Karlsefni's voyage was the last time the Vikings would try to make a permanent settlement in the new land. People still sometimes wonder why. After all, the land was rich and fruitful. The climate was mild. The answer is quite simple. The Vikings had no guns. Their swords and knives were sharp. Yet they were no match for the Indians' deadly arrows.

Much later, when men from Spain, England, and France came to North America, the Indians were defeated by their strange "sticks that spit fire."

CHAPTER 6

The Sister

Leif had no more brothers. But he still had a sister. Freydis had Erik the Red's blood flowing through her veins. She was, if anything, more heartless and cruel than her father had ever been.

One day Freydis met two men from Iceland. Helgi and Finnbogi were brothers on a trading voyage. Freydis saw their well-built ship in the harbor. An idea struck her. Maybe the brothers would go to Vinland with her. She spoke to them about it. It did not take long for them to agree.

There would be two ships. One was owned by Helgi and Finnbogi. One was owned by Freydis. Each ship would carry 30 men plus any women who wanted to go along. Freydis did not live up to this plan. One dark night she slipped five extra men onto her ship. She wanted her crew to be stronger in case of trouble.

They had no plans to settle in the new country. They agreed that Freydis and the brothers would split profits 50-50. They hoped to return from Vinland with ships crammed with timber, grapes, and fur.

Before leaving, Freydis asked Leif to sell her his Vinland houses. Once again he said no. But he was willing to lend them to her.

The ocean voyage was not an easy one. Helgi and Finnbogi got to Vinland before Freydis. Their crew unloaded their ship. Then they carried their gear up to Leif's houses. When Freydis got there, she was furious.

"You have no right to be in my brother's houses," she screamed. "He lent them to *me*."

It was easier to give in than to argue. Helgi and Finnbogi packed up their gear and moved near a small lake. There they built their own big hall and huts. From time to time during the winter the two groups would argue.

At last they stopped speaking to one another altogether.

Early one spring morning Freydis went to see Finnbogi at his house. She said she wanted to talk to him. She had a favor to ask. She wanted to leave Vinland and go home, she told him. But she needed a big ship to carry the load of timber her men had cut. Could she use the larger ship owned by Finnbogi and his brother?

Finnbogi thought it over. Then he agreed. It was a good way to get rid of Freydis. Perhaps then they could have some peace. He said goodbye and went back to bed.

Poor Finnbogi! He should never have

trusted Freydis. She rushed back to her camp and woke her men. She told them that the two brothers had beaten her. They had to be harshly punished, she said. Her men rushed to the brothers' huts on the lake. Everyone was still sleeping. They had little chance to defend themselves.

One by one the stunned men were bound and taken outside. One by one they were killed. Five women were left. Freydis ordered her men to kill them. They would not do it. She grabbed an axe and did the evil deed herself.

Freydis had to keep the massacre a secret. She made her crew promise never to tell what had happened. Instead they would say that the 35 murdered people had chosen to stay in Vinland.

"I will kill any man who tells what took place," she thundered. And, indeed, the men knew she would do just that.

And so Freydis returned to Greenland. Her ship was bursting with cargo. Her profits were high. She paid her crew well. Then she returned to her farm to lead a quiet life.

Such a life was not to be. Some of the crew members could not keep the awful secret. Soon stories of what had happened reached Leif. He could not believe his ears. "I must find out the truth," he vowed. He had three men from Freydis's crew brought to him. They were beaten until the whole terrible story came out. Then he let them go. But what to do about Freydis?

"I have not the heart to punish my sister as she deserves," Leif said. "All I can say is that she and her family will never prosper." From that time on, Freydis and her husband and her children were shunned by everyone in Greenland. No one spoke to them. No one bought their crops.

What about Leif? Was he also shunned because of his sister's acts? We do not know. The saga of Leif Eriksson ends here.